"*Green Mountain Zen* renders the cycles of the human spirit as it surrenders to the shortest, most shut-down days of winter, keeping the coals of itself aglow, and then opens to celebration as the earth softens, greens, and again offers its abundance. This is a wise book, attentive to the nuances of inner and outer weather in a way that might best be called devotional — patient and deeply respectful. Image by image — Romaine seeds 'the size of a baby's eyelash,' the raindrop 'that lingers/ like a diamond in the cup of the lupine's fan-shape leaf'— Demers renders the *feel* of seasons, much as Chinese painters did through spare, careful brush strokes. This is the perfect book to dream with beside a warm fire, or overlooking a harvest-ready garden while morning sun is still fresh and cool."

— Leslie Ullman, poet whose most recent books are
Library of Small Happiness and *Progress on the Subject of Immensity*

"The poems in *Green Mountain Zen* by Michelle Demers are original in a way that really matters: they speak clearly of their source, inseparable from the pure current of their language. They have an effect like afternoon light hitting ordinary objects: they illuminate, clarify, and direct our gaze toward *the ordinary magic* of what we love but often overlook. Minding and mining the details of her particular landscape, *What is hope, after all, if not the idea of crocus and tulip, / if not the brown hare feeding in the early morning in Vermont?* Michelle leads us to the river of spirit that flows through and beneath all seasons; these poems of the body in place connect us to the world. I read them with care and admiration for each one is a sensory delight and an inspiration."

— Mary Kay Rummel, Author of *Cypher Garden* and
The Lifeline Trembles, Former poet laureate of Ventura County, CA

"*Green Mountain Zen* is a cycle of poems devoted to witnessing the immediate natural world. Stilling herself amid the winds of ceaseless human chaos, Demers' poems find the ordinary joys and riches of nature before her. Beginning in the lean light of November, as she leads us into her 'winter-dark' corner in the Northeast, her poems use direct accessible lyrics as they chart progressive changes in weather and temperature, noticing, for example, how the willow outside her window is glazed alternately with ice and then snow making it look like 'a chandelier,/ then a powdered wig.'"

As she watches a grey sun rise over 'silent white fields' and anticipates 'raucous daffodils/making their way to the surface,' her poems look at the majesty and mystery of the semi urban, semi rural Vermont landscape the way Rilke studied the caged panther. The result is a duet with ever-present nature, whose lyrics she scores in a variety of poetic forms — haiku, pantoum, free verse, ghazal, concrete poetry.

Green Mountain Zen acts like a mindfulness almanac, as Demers' poems pose poignant questions and notice a variety of answers growing, thawing, ripening, rising and falling around her. She both wonders, 'How can this moment/ break open/ the sunflower seed?' and discovers that the cawing crow splits 'frozen air into particles, shattering' her inner chatter 'like a koan'— and that's what this lovely collection will do for you."

— Julia Shipley, author of *The Academy of Hay*, winner of the 2015 Melissa Lanitis Gregory Poetry Prize and a finalist for the 2016 Vermont Book Award

Green Mountain Zen

Poems by

Michelle Demers

BLUE LIGHT PRESS ◆ 1ST WORLD PUBLISHING

1ST WORLD
PUBLISHING

SAN FRANCISCO ◆ FAIRFIELD ◆ DELHI

Green Mountain Zen

Copyright ©2019 by Michelle Demers

1st World Library
PO Box 2211
Fairfield, IA 52556
www.1stworldpublishing.com

Blue Light Press
www.bluelightpress.com
bluelightpress@aol.com

Book & Cover Art & Design
Melanie Gendron
melaniegendron999@gmail.com

Cover Art
Artwork courtesy of Ronalee Crocker

Author Photo
Up Country Photography

First Edition

Library of Congress Control Number: 2019935301

ISBN 9781421836249

With ongoing gratitude

to all my teachers

We don't remember days,
We remember moments.

— Cesare Pavese

Contents

Into Darkness

Into the Light

Into Darkness

Into Darkness

Toward November
mornings begin late and cold
with a thin sheet of ice on the bird bath.
Finches exchange their exuberant gold
for a sensible brown,
and the field mice
ready their burrows. Each morning
I find myself sleeping later,
pulled toward a hibernation I must resist, or risk
losing vital time to work, to live.

Still, the longer nights serve to tamp down
my manic frenzy, the hysterical leftovers
of an over-caffeinated world.
And despite its reputation, darkness
soothes the cranked-up life lived at warp speed.

Welcome, darkness. Wrap us in the comfort
of the coming winter when we can rest,
take in the solstice, absorb strength from silence.

And after the dark lifts, we will re-emerge,
and walk forward with bouquets of fire in our hands.

Fallow

Quiet settles in with shorter days
and chillier nights. Leaves blown onto the forest floor
provide bedding for the doe, protection
for the field mouse and vole.
Most of the geese have left.

An occasional mild November day
still appears when grasshopper
and garter snake enjoy thinning sun.
Black and copper woolly bear caterpillars inch
their way to the winter safety of leaf piles and logs.

The garden rests — no broccoli, no carrots.
This is the time nature beckons us
to go within to find what we were made of
before the noise of toil and bustle
made us forget.

This is the month of my birth. I know
this silence in the pit of my reptilian brain.
It reminds me each year after the fallen leaves, before
the snow, why I must return again
and again to the deep replenishing.

Migration

*There's a beauty in the world, though it's harsher
than we ever expect it to be.*

> — Michael Cunningham

In the early winter morning, I watch
the filmy dawn lift. Birds I can't see
fuss and chirp in my chimney, already making plans
for spring. Outside, thick snowflakes
plummet down like stones, but leave
no sound. I think of all the years
my life felt weighed down
by events beyond my control.
I want to be the willow, shaking
the hoar frost from its spindly, fragile
branches. In the brightening sky I imagine
the wild birds logging thousands of miles
on muscular wings, risking everything, long necks
driving forward into the wind.

Killing Frost

Who can say at what point dying begins?
— Bia Lowe

This morning the season's first thick frost
silences remaining field mice, chipmunks
and meadow voles, driving them beneath the earth.
Any lingering flowers, even
the hardy mums, are burned brown.

The cold wakes us with its cutting
chill, then makes the early end of day
seem even darker. We forget sweat
and sunburn. We can't feel
our fingers, and focus only on the murmur
of our heartbeats that seem to have slowed
for hibernation.

Gorgeous, terrifying, frost crystals
cover the tall grasses of wild fields as though
each frozen drop were positioned like a mandala.
Soon, with the rising winter sun,
they too will be dismantled,
wrapped in silken air
and returned to the ephemeral world.

December

This is the taste of what has been lost,
crushed by the heaviness of winter skies.
I am a daughter of the dark Earth.
Everything must be forgiven like debts.

Crushed by the heaviness of winter skies
we gradually wear away our false outer skins.
Everything must be forgiven like debts.
A tang of black tea lingers in the throat.

We gradually wear away our false outer skins.
After all, how is happiness created?
A tang of black tea lingers in the throat,
like a slow walk through bare maple groves.

Above all, how is happiness created?
I am a daughter of the dark Earth.
I walk slowly through bare maple groves.
This is the taste of what has been lost.

Snap

We haven't felt a cold this deep in years,
not this eye-tearing, face-numbing, pipe-bursting cold of Vermont.

When wool-hatted heads are lowered, shoulders raised
against the bone-freezing winds of Vermont.

The finches puff out their winter-brown feathers,
the Labradors dance to protect paws in the steely cold of Vermont.

Nights, I sleep in wooly socks and huddle under flannel
while endless darkness tells the story of Vermont.

The company of stars and Wolf Moon keep me from shattering
amid harsh fields of ice and stoic mountains of Vermont.

In the morning, sub-zero temps turn the air whitish gray.
A magnificent calm defines itself: Vermont.

In my mind I plan the spring garden that today
lies hard and frozen under dried autumn leaves of Vermont.

Will early spinach rise when the frozen ground thaws?
The soil will answer: survival is the promise of Vermont.

What is hope, after all, if not the idea of crocus and tulip,
if not the brown hare feeding in the early morning in Vermont?

And what of the long stretches of silence that echo
Michelle in my dreams? Is it nirvana? Or Vermont?

Messages

Night blizzards when landscape disappears
leave me feeling buried alive. I burrow
under a down quilt trying to obliterate
wind that vibrates my window,
forcing entry through sliver-cracks
in tiny atonal screams.

It could be a dream,
but I look through the glass and see
a holographic shape of a man,
fierce snow flying all around him.
It could be God. It could be
Obi-Wan. He shouts into the wild night
words that disappear into the howling
and a thin music evaporates
from his lips.

The harmony, though gone,
ripples through my lungs
and around me the air
suddenly grows dense and humid
as though a presence
wraps itself around me.

In the morning I will remember only
remnants, hoarse shivers
that force themselves from my throat,
as the gray sun
rises over silent white fields.

Blinded

I sit in the dark hole
of January, where the day's peripheral vision
is blocked and the tunnel upward
dull and cloudy, a cataracted eye.
The knowledge that every day will lengthen
at dawn and dusk lifts the heart, but
microscopically.

While I'm at my desk in early morning
sipping jasmine tea, the black square
of my window yields no sign
of roaming deer whose tracks
I will spot later in the day, no sign
of rabbit-killing foxes
who leave bloodstains in the snow,
no sign of snow-laden pines
flailing under frigid winds.

A vase of tiny yellow roses
transports me to softening earth,
tulips thrusting skyward, grape hyacinths
taunting hungry deer and rabbits.
In my mind Shasta daisies
multiply magically under a gentle
sun, and hummingbirds
return, their iridescent green backs
streaking the air. Now
when the sun flares up
on this January morning, a cardinal
quivering with song
greets me from the naked branches
of the mountain ash. Suddenly
the tree is aflame.

Acting As If

I want to be seduced by spring
waiting in the wings even though
in this winter-dark corner
of the Northeast, it is mid-January.

Despite the thaw that brought
heavy rains, fog, and temps that strangely
rose with the altitude, we all know
winter is still on stage
about to project its piercing voice again.

Soon bone-chilling cold, knee-high
snow, and early darkness will return to hog
the show. But today I walk in a spotlight
of sun, booted feet squishing
the spongy ground covered in brown
flattened grasses.

For a few brief moments, I relax my shoulders,
remembering the fragrant apple blossoms and the brilliant
gold of the finch.

Into the Vast

For two hours now
midday sun hidden behind
      snowclouds
clings to the idea of warmth,
             even in February
when stones hold tight to silence
and mountains
      show inexhaustible patience with
      rime ice and jet stream winds.

As though blessing us
      clouds finally part
signaling storm's end.
          We begin to let
our shoulders drop, and breathe in
      whatever energy we can
      from the glow.

Fortified by a thin radiance,
      we pick ourselves up,
      gather the power of fire within
          and move forward into the vast
               illumination
undaunted by the knowledge
that the way forward
      could blind us
even as it lights our path.

In Winter

Skin: parched, needing vats
of rose petal moisturizer.
Never enough.

The haiku of outdoors:
everything compacted into ice.
Throat: scratchy. Head: fuzzy.
Sky: flat, indiscriminate,
one solid cloud.
Me: on the verge of Prozac.

Cat: cabin fevered, watching
snowflakes swirl.
Me: sipping hot tea
with names like "Tazo Calm"
and "Breathe Deep."

Each day: sunset one minute later.
The willow outside:
a chandelier,
then a powdered wig.

Afternoon slides into night,
one darkness into another.
I listen to Norah Jones,
trying to get my sexy back.

Practice: wait
as though I were a tulip bulb
buried in the deep frozen ground
holding fast to red-petal winds
and slow, liquid songs.

Now

I want nothing more
than to stay inside on this white and frozen
day and listen to the comforting
sounds of home: humming humidifier,
heater whooshing warm air,
washing machine whirring, chugging, spinning.
But my mind keeps racing ahead
to the coming day, eating it up like a hungry
Labrador: papers to grade,
bills to pay, beds to make, research to do.

All I want is now, opening out to itself,
revealing worlds inside worlds
where all that exists is one
black and white downy woodpecker
tapping at the suet, or the joyful pine
dancing a tango with the chill wind,
swallowing hours, days, the sweep
of time itself.

Soon I will glance at my to-do list, check off
one or two things and move
toward the next item.
And behind me, the moment waits,
perching and gliding forever
until I am ready to return.

Buried

under
six inches of heavy
wet snow piled on top of
twenty inches of airy dry snow.
Buried in aching backs and heating pads
and Extra Strength Tylenol. Beneath hours at the
computer reading badly written student essays. Buried in cat
fur and laundry, in bank statements and bills. Buoyed by hearty stews
and thick blankets, long warm nights of hugs and dreams. Lifted in blessings and
galaxies sparkling in headlight beams. Embraced by benevolence, floating on silent snow.

The Easing

In the frozen heart of winter
she watches from the kitchen window
as hungry chickadees and house finches
feast on sunflower seeds
from tubular feeders. Now
and then, full frontal jaybirds
and downy woodpeckers claim
their share of thistle and suet.

She watches as Rilke watched
the panther in his cage
move fluidly back and forth
holding prison in his eyes.

How the body carries
lifetimes of sadness
in shoulders, neck, and back.
As finches flit and perch
she dreams of tender shoots
of grass and profuse pink blossoms
and slowly releases
what was trapped in her spine,
a thousand doves.

Field Guide to Survival

Heart, dressed in white feathers,
surrounded by grey bones of trees,
wonders how to survive in winter.
Mind, clothed in worn-out sweaters,
says it's all about layers that trap air.
Rhododendron leaves curl tight as cigarettes
against sub-zero temps.
A white sky cruel and fierce
hides sunrise behind snow clouds.
Deer press heart-shaped tracks
in snow under cover of darkness.

In snow under cover of darkness,
deer press heart-shaped tracks
while sunrise waits behind snow clouds.
A white sky cruel and fierce
against sub-zero temps
curls rhododendron leaves like cigarettes
because it's all about layers that trap air.
Mind, clothed in worn out sweaters
wonders about survival in winter.
Surrounded by grey bones of trees,
heart bursts in white feathers.

Crow Medicine

Three degrees with harsh north winds
make my eyebrows burn as I step
out the door at sunrise. Beyond the deck, a crow
perches in the willow. Black crow.
Black branch outlined against a brightening sky.
Soon, another crow settles, their glossy black backs
turned to me. They squat like two old men on a park bench
discussing the country's sagging economy,
the high price of gasoline.

I watch and wonder
at the crow's ability to stay warm
against nature's savage bite.
Bundled in thick layers against
the bitterness, I hear the familiar
caw in the treetops and look up to see the flapping
as crow moves from one branch to another.
I think of a shaman who shapeshifted into a crow,
announcing the courage we all share, to enter into
darkness in search of the sun.

Magnolia Oolong in February

For my Minnesota friend Ting Ting

Here is the three-foot drift on the back deck
     from the Valentine's Day blizzard
Here the ferocious blue sky, left clean
     and flawless after two days of blinding white
And here are the calls of the chickadee
     in the frigid cold, unseen, but alive
Snow tracks of small brown rabbits
     leading toward the birch tree
Burgundy sumac seeds, like drops of blood
     enfolding latent life
And here is the shadow lengthening later each day,
     reaching toward spring
Cardinal in the bare brown branches,
     a tiny flame in a dark landscape
Inside, sleeping cat in a pool
     of sunshine on the couch
One magenta blossom growing
     from the Christmas cactus, alone, radiant
A cup of sweet magnolia oolong,
     blossoming with the flavor of far-off friendship
The silence that widens with each breath,
     drifting, lost inside itself
And here is a stack of work left undone
     because the world is too magnificent to overlook

Trying to Escape Winter,
I Go to the Greenhouse

Water splashes on water
and a sexy bromeliad blooms scarlet
like a mutant clitoris
showing off in front of
the demure bonsai trees,
Japanese in their politeness.
Overhead the massive yucca
looms, tangled in greenhouse netting,
trying to make its escape.
Lavish pink hydrangeas
pretend a wedding procession
while gangly violet orchids
fail to hide their astonishing tenderness.

Only a few hours away
a Nor'easter barrels up the East Coast, carrying
heavy snows that threaten to blur
the landscape white yet again, twisting
spring's arm behind its back
for just one more week.

Cabin Fever

The thermometer suctioned to my glass doors
broke last week.
Was it the long stretch of sub-zero nights
or the sudden shift to mid-winter mildness
that shattered the mercury?

Outside, flakes return.
This time they're so tiny, I have to strain
to be sure it's really snowing again.
I draw the drapes to avoid being buried
in backed-up desperation.

If darkness comes before I am ready,
will it soothe or frighten?
If God traces my name in the snow,
then blows a wind over it,
will I never get to smell the hyacinths?
If relief falls from the sky
in the shape of a raven, will my heart
recognize it as the gift it is? If night clouds
speak to me in whispers, will they set free
the music of the stars and drown out
the low hum of hibernation?

Valentine's Day

In the frigid February dawn
she sees the air itself
hanging suspended in a grayish haze
like a doe hyper-alert for predators
while confident crows strut
boldly on the fierce crust
with their bloodless survivor's feet,
pecking at invisible food.

The world is locked in, paralyzed
by blind cycles of brutality and suffering.

She yearns to wrap herself
in doeskin and leap
through snowy fields
leaving only tracks, deep mystery,
listening for sounds of raucous daffodils
making their way to the surface, pushing
for light with everything they've got.

Winter Walk

My boots crunch on squeaky snow
but all other sounds are muted, smothered.
Above the silence and the footsteps
my thoughts whisper while I
walk in the middle of the day.
Urgently they say we are meant
to make sense of the world alone. But they lie.
We connect with each other by design
or lucky accident. At the end of the road
a huge blackbird lifts, its caws splitting
the frozen air into particles,
shattering my inner chatter
like a koan. For a fraction of a second
my breath stops, the wide onyx wings
shoot through the white landscape,
transporting us both
straight into the center of this life.

When the light returns

Lake Champlain is still frozen, and no finches
wear their spring gold. But there is a barely detectable
softness on some days that can be taken deep
into the lungs without pain. Mornings creep in
at 6:30 instead of 7, and daylight
lasts well past 5 pm. But the back
of winter is not yet broken. No buds
dare crack open, no crocuses break ground

though hope hangs on the few moments
of lengthening light each day, on the snowmelt
from a weak but hardworking sun.
We wonder if there's strength enough
for the last bit of the season, the most
difficult part when we are winter-weary
and have had enough of wrinkled root vegetables.
We wonder when the lifting will come
and we will greet the new earth
that we thought had forgotten us.

Off Kilter

Only mid-February, barely sugaring time
but early warmth forces asphalt
to crack and mound, jolting my car
as though I drive through a post-war battlefield.
My mission: fresh asparagus and bitter greens.

Winter has somehow glided by
without its usual fierceness this year.
Little snow. Little sub-zero.
It makes me ache even more deeply
for languid summer days
when it's too hot to move,
for cicadas and katydids
trilling, rasping, buzzing
their metallic, mesmerizing field concertos.
That is still five months away.

Each day lengthens by two whole minutes now
in this northern hemisphere, and half a dozen
small yellow shoots near my front door
poke through bare, unfrozen ground normally
covered by snow. I dream of daffodils, tulips, irises,
fields of black-eyed Susans. I want to drown
in lilacs, forsythia, pussy willows, hyacinths,
narcissus. I am ecstatic for orchids,
frangipani, bougainvillia.

But outside my window the ugly brown lawn
reminds me that the march of seasons
is deliberate, perfectly timed.
So I clutch my thick wooly sweater,
savor the slowness as the sap

trickles out of sugar maples
and force some paper whites
until the thrilling perfume
blooms my heart once again.

March, on Stage

Swirling snowdevils,
clouds of white smoke
        exploding from ground to air,
ghostly dancers taking shape,
        dissolving in seconds —
the entire landscape shifts and whirls like a river.

My hands pass over the warm mound
        of black and white cat fur,
        silky and vibrating in my lap.
We watch the end of winter
        trying violently
        to hang on.

House entrance blocked by drifts.
Walkway not shoveled, rock salt container
        in need of refilling. Chores
        will have to wait until the storm's end.
For now, nature's show
        mesmerizes us. We'll stay until
        the final number and maybe even
        the encore.

To the Snows of Early Spring

After Li Ch'Ing-Chao, Sung Dynasty (960-1279 AD)

Thin gray skies
> Thick ice
> clings to roadside cliffs
Patches of brown grass
> beneath tiny snowflakes

Even though light
> now floods
> end of day

Daffodils
> bloom briefly
> wilt swiftly
Regret
Tastes like bitter greens
> this brief life
How can this moment
> break open
> the sunflower seed?

Sugaring Time

To soothe your cold, I feed you warm liquids and oatmeal,
oatmeal with raisins and love and maple syrup,
syrup made from sap dripping from trees in a sugarbush
just when we're about to celebrate the breaking,
the breaking apart of a long winter, thinking maybe,
maybe we've both escaped just in time with our sanity
and health knitted together, when we force ourselves
not to look out the windows anymore,
the windows that keep revealing white
and white and gray and white and brown,
crushed brown matted grass flooded by snowmelt,
flooding your sensibilities and sinuses,
sinuses clogged now on Friday night,
the night that begins the first weekend in spring.

Deer in a March Meadow

A calm sunny morning
for late winter in the Northeast
when high winds carrying snow
grow common. I enjoy a walk
on a dirt road between the fast-moving
Winooski River and a fenced-off nature preserve.
In the distance, three wild turkeys,
their hulking, slow-moving backs
easy to identify. Beaks to the ground,
they forage for insects and grasses,
whatever clings to life
this time of year. Beyond the turkeys,
a small deer herd grazes, intent
on finding food in the matted brown field.

Two workmen in pick-ups stop on the road
to peer at the deer and turkeys through binoculars.
One offers me a gaze, bringing the animals
up close. I remember once touching
a young abandoned deer a friend had saved
from starvation. I lay my hand
on that trusting creature's tawny coat,
felt its oily denseness
and sensed in that moment the meaning
of my own white-tailed wildness.

Season of Persistence

Last day of winter looks
exactly like the first day of spring:
dull, cold, severe, the sun
hidden behind pewter clouds.
We wring our hands and moan,
wondering how we can bear another day,
another week of single digits.

Robins do not have the luxury of anguish.
They must feed. Now. A sea of these
red-breasteds forages beneath the apple tree
extracting food from last year's withered droppings
because no juicy earthworms, beetles or grubs
are thawed yet from frozen ground.

Today, we pray for the resilience of robins,
admire the grace, the patience, the steadfastness,
and take a lesson to move forward
without complaint or judgment,
taking what is offered as nature begins
the slow dance of spring.

Into the Light

Green Mountain Zen

The roads crack open with frost heaves, white
with dried salt, swollen from melting snow
then refrozen, asphalt bulging.

In the air above naked trees
a woodpecker, its head blazing,
fights warming winds
in the slow light of morning.

Wood ducks navigate the river's ice floes
in a treacherous current
and no words are strong enough
to stop the world from thawing.

In the near distance, dark blue
storm clouds threaten
the persistence of wind chills.
March is the month of melancholy
with its roadside snow, dirty and tired

yet buried beneath, white trilliums sleep
each with their three shy petals waiting
for their moment, brilliant
and forgiving.

Resilience

After W.S. Merwin

Thank you long-needled pine
that can withstand the weight
of winter ice. Thank you
for the ordinary magic
      of silent peepers
      under frozen cattails
for sweetness of winter birdsong
for the sugar maple's deeply furrowed bark
      how it protects the heartwood
      how I must do the same
thank you for wind's welcome taste
      a reminder that breath heals
      every moment
thank you my secret center
that must play its music loudly now
in hopes of drowning out
the demagogue who
threatens to extinguish
the world's goodness
how else could I survive what is to come

Fires Start in the Heart

I write nightly letters to God:
Please let me know my rightful place
on earth. Don't let me get discouraged.
Mornings, I watch the first rains
of the new spring season
wash this littered earth.
Small buds and tender shoots
of tulips and daffodils poke up through
broken branches and dead leaves
under a thin new moon. Return
of red-winged blackbirds.
Awakening of bears. I feel the hold
the outside world has on me —
winter, the grip of ice and darkness — spring,
the quickening of life, frozen earth melting to mud.

Today on winter's departure, I look at maples
stripped of leaves, color, growth,
but yielding clear sap. I imagine
green, blossoms, and nesting sparrows.
In the long silence of afternoon, the ache
in my cervical spine tells me it's time for winds
to clear the season's detritus, to blow through
the vertebrae and whoosh out leaves, broken
branches and leavings of fox, groundhog, and rabbit.

In the quiet of the day, long-needled evergreens
shed woody cones, their seed-scattering complete.
I neglect my work to breathe in the aftermath
of frenzied occupation, too many words moving
through crevices of my mind. I remind myself
that afternoon will slip into night as it has
a million times a million, that I will go with it,
that fires start in the heart and I must
wish myself well again and again.

Weather Report: March 20

The day is equinoxed with squalls. One is a loosely woven fabric,
       one a sap moon. We explore the earth like peepers
            awakening hollowed and anxious. The night is
tight and hoary. The night is a fox. Before us, a slippery patron
       of hunger. Bring us a mild cup of fennel tea. We have few
            spongy carrots left in the bin. We do not ask,
although we lick our lips. Maples are squeezed by plastic tubing.
       Our names are mountain, mole, and hare. We travel
            the still-congealed ground
and try to breathe the soil.

Against All Odds

And what comes before the fragile blossom
of the snowdrop? Of course, it's the bud, the stem,
the shoot, the seed; but what before that?
The flower itself, the downy petals and sexual stamen,
the stiff stem, tender shoot that may be devoured
by ravenous winter-starved deer, rabbits
and mice; then the seed, snugged in moist darkness
that itself can be nibbled upon by moles, insects, worms.
The miracle, the mind-boggling, stupefying,
inconceivable miracle is that this flower,
any flower, survives at all to wave and breathe,
to spread its perfume and seeds, even if only
for a day, an hour, an everlasting moment.

The Crossing

After the return of fox sparrows
comes spring migration of salamanders,
finger-length, lizard-like,
moving en masse from upland woods
to vernal spawning pools.
Blue-spotted, yellow-spotted,
slug-eating beings defying night-slicked roads
on four-toed feet by the hundreds
to get where they must.
Many will not survive.

Kind human souls armed with flashlights
and slickers dare to face darkness and rain
to escort them to safety.

I think about the "salamander schedule"
and the pace of my own quotidian life.
We both risk unknown dangers. Yet to live bravely
takes blind trust. And perhaps
it is possible that a gentle hand from above
will lift us and get us to the other side
of the killing highway.

Red

After Charles Wright

Red is for waking up, the jolt, the blood recognition:
the blackbird's wing, that red, the return of light;
heart music, the red of obsession;
the red of foxes, their red backs;
the fierce red of birth;
clairvoyant red, the red of sunrise;
the unexpected red, singing for her and for him;
the red of Mars, not far from a waning gibbous moon;
the red of what is miraculous;
red of peony, red of claw;
the red of motion, the red inside arteries;
the red of berries, their wine stain;
sumac red, furry seeds;
the red of the cardinal, the water, the open door.

Balm

Stiff after days of turning soil, shoveling
compost, raking dark clumps into
fine tilth, the gardener reclines inside
as rain soaks the ground. The cold
wet spring will soon yield
to long days thick with weeds and bugs
and hot dry spells with no rain. But
today she daydreams seeds
in their singular shapes —
flat white ovals for squash, dark
bumpy beads for beets, tiny grayish
slivers for greens — all sown
into a healthy patch of earth
smelling of loam and rich
possibilities of ripened cucumbers,
kale, cilantro, parsley.
The aches in her bones
will soon surrender
to the season's harvest, each stalk,
leaf and fruit a gift, soothing.

The Immensity

waits inside the geranium for the hummingbird to come with
its invisible wings, its vibrations and needle beak
(ready for red)

waits while apple trees count their leaves and organize their
cells for the most aggregate sunlight
(canopy maintenance)

waits while finches swirl, robins weave and feather nests, worms
squidge through rain-soaked soil
(domestic yearnings)

for grass seeds to free their blades, carry the wayward ant,
thicken like the fur of the panther
(low-lying jungle)

waits while cats dream of voles tunneling beneath the surface

(twitching fur)

waits beyond the clouds, keeping track of flight patterns of
geese pushing through the vibrating air
(global positioning)

on the other side of midnight inside the heartbeat of the falcon,
beyond the secrets of wings
(widening the edges)

Too Early for Planting

Today I will dream of dinnerplate dahlias
all showy and sensual.
I will inspect the papery gladioli bulbs
and wonder if my poor rocky soil can nourish
enough to push up the tall, ruffled blossoms.
Today I will run my hands over seed packets
of lupine, zinnia, coreopsis, poppy
and reject those that say Zone 6-8.
For here in Zone 4, we like the words
hardy and *frost resistant*. Here our season begins
after Memorial Day when first come
the small beaks eating new seeds. Then
the rabbits, groundhogs and deer with mincing teeth
and hungry bellies. Then come slugs
and beetles, rampant and busy. The zinnias
will survive and maybe the poisonous lupines.
I will protect the gladioli and dahlias
with soap and cayenne pepper.
I will watch the flowers rise
as they defy gravity and pests and beasts
with razor teeth. And one day when the sun
is full out and three moon cycles have passed,
the brilliance of petal and sepal, stamen, leaves
and stem will blast their beauty
like a mirage, creating waves of dense
velvet color that grow straight
into my perennial heart.

First of May

Rushing through life,
gulping bad food, sleeping
too briefly, sleeping too fitfully,
racing to complete in a day
tasks that need a week.
But then sudden greenness
of new grass, waves of heady
spring fragrance, small pink blossoms,
the *whoit whoit whoit whoit*
of the invisible cardinal in the willow
awakens me, tells me it's okay
to breathe again, be held
in the arms of morning.

Planting Peas

Early May still acts like March.
Cold winds, cloudy skies, muddy ground.
Yesterday, as I pulled weeds and shoveled compost,
a light snow began to fall, confirming the chill
in my bones. But I stuck it out
another hour before heading inside
for hot tea and a warm shower.

Today, no snow, but a forecast of rain
as I loosen winter-hardened soil
for planting, then push pea seeds
into small holes with frigid fingers.

Above me two red-tailed hawks soar
in slow circles on broad, fringed wings.
One issues a call that rips the greying air.
It flings my attention from earth
to sky, and for a moment
I am lifted, not breathing,
aware only of the silence left behind.

What Brings Us to Our Knees?

A mother robin nesting in the rhododendron,
the anxious worry, the gray raining skies
day after day, the crush and burn of us,
our quotidian lives, broken sleep,
our powdery thoughts.

The drunk dance of the bumblebee, first
barefoot steps in new grass, our wormy toes
and bony knees, our hunger for meaning,
our seedlings hiding below the surface,
our calm exteriors and rippling interiors.

What drops us to the damp earth,
makes us collapse at the spring-green of buds,
and what buckles our stance
when the first hummingbird
arrives to drink the nectar?

Who will see the crumpled pile of us,
the aching joy of us? Who will
smell the lilacs when we
erupt with wonder?

The Softening

With steel rake, hoe and spade,
I hack away at the garden's winter-tightened clods of earth
using winter-softened shoulders, back, and arms
till sweat pours from every pore.
I shovel compost, mix it in,
chop and sift and rake some more
until the soil is rich and dark and loamy,
with tilth of fine black pearls,
a bed so luxurious
any seed would be blessed to lie in it.

When I stop to mop my face and neck
I hear the clear, unmistakable song of the cardinal
who hides behind tender new leaves.
Only song fills me.

I sow the early crops: radish, lettuce,
peas, spinach. Making a shallow dent with my hoe's edge,
I drop in Romaine seeds the size of a baby's eyelash,
tuck them in and sigh at the loveliness
of evenly spaced rows marked by stake and string.

Tomorrow, my muscles will ache
and I will rest as spring rains forecast for five days
begin the awakening.

Garden Journal: Three Haiku

Large, round pea seeds
planted deep, two inches apart
love cold soil.

Red admiral butterfly
visits while I plant squash.
He flirts, I rest.

I set large tomato cages
over small young seedlings.
Soon they'll try to escape.

Lifting the Curtain

1.

The cat's ghost sleeps in her favorite spot.
The sun illumines a newly washed earth
after the thunderstorms.
Count the chipmunks — three — eating seeds
and know they tunneled the holes
near the azalea bush. No surprise
when the cardinal wakes the world at 5 am.
Tell me a story, a voice sings back.

2.

A robin issues a sharp call.
In the distance, a faint response.
June is moist and fertile,
the mother of a million seeds.
The lightning — in a flash, the face
of the universe.

3.

We are part of something vast,
consuming and faintly blue-violet,
the color of transcendence.
Bacopa cascade in a flower box on the deck.
Lobelia edge the garden
between deep red geraniums.
Traffic noises far off from the road.
Fat bumblebee works the pollen.
We are love itself, piercing
the sky beyond thin clouds.

Cottonwood Seeds

In the light the missing earring is found
In the light the radish glows wettish red
In the light the bee carries an extra load of pollen
In the light the lettuce leaves freshen
In the light the calla lily turns in acceptance
In the light blue veins appear where they were not
In the light the tea tastes sweeter
In the light the flea resettles in the field
In the light the water magnifies the leaf
In the light the dog pees (again) on the flower bed
In the light the grackle shatters droplets in the bird bath
In the light fluffs of cottonwood seeds
helicopter into the field like snow

Hummingbird

Instructions for living a life:
Pay attention
Be astonished.
Tell about it. — Mary Oliver

Whirring at 30 miles per hour
she zips to the feeder
wings ablur, hovering
up, down, with
exquisite control
then dips her needle beak,
long and slightly curved.

As quickly as she comes, she leaves,
her miniature heart racing at 1200 beats per minute.
I wonder where she goes,
where her walnut-sized nest
hangs in high branches,
lined with spider silk and dandelion down.
She will lay her pea-sized eggs
and raise the chicks alone.
They will grow larger than she
by the time they fledge. Yet come fall
she will have the strength
to fly to the Caribbean, cross the Gulf of Mexico
in one flight that will take nearly 20 hours.

As I watch her from my porch
with my elderly cat who grows thinner
each week, I marvel at
the world's heart-breaking persistence.

After the Rains

After a cloudy, rain-filled week, cold and seed-discouraging,
the sun has emerged. Screeches, chirps, and songs
of every neighboring bird
      rise in full voice

          Today, I see six ruby-throats
at the feeder and many more of their mates in lesser plumage.
Today, the cat naps unmoving on the outside table
next to my books and my dancing pen, her brown
tail-tip lifting and lowering as though on its own.
          Today I am glad for the shimmering
coppery rosebush leaves and the tiny
new radish sprouts that look like butterflies.
Tender lettuce leaves have taken root
      and a droplet of rain lingers
      like a diamond in the cup of the lupine's fan-shaped leaf.

Life goes on after burials,
      plant-damaging frost, and mile-thick
      clouds that hang around for a week.
This, this is the reward for letting go
of each moment without hurrying for the next.

Strawberry Moon

Finally, frost
suspends its nightly rounds, and the young
tomatoes and beet greens relax
in their snug soil beds. The cilantro
need no longer fear
the white claws of night.
It is the time
of the strawberry moon,
a name the Algonquins gave to herald the arrival
of the heart-shaped fruit.

Is there ever a time
when some fear is never present?

While cold kills instantly, slugs and beetles
administer a slow death, munching
their mean holes
in radish and romaine.

Is it possible to forgive the ravages
of weather and pestilence?
Must we remain at their mercy?

Until we find answers, we cover the young plants
when the frost warnings come. We offer
the slugs a cup of Pabst Blue Ribbon
to entice them away from the delicious
lunch of greenery, and wink at the strawberry
moon in a toast to a temporary truce.

Renewal

I plod out to the early morning garden,
mug of tea in hand
as though to talk to an old friend.

I murmur praise to the newly formed
green globes of the Big Boy, cheer on
the overachieving zucchini, thank
the Brussels sprouts that persevere
despite the wet spring
and onslaught of slugs.

I bend my face close to the feathery
carrot tops and promise I will thin them soon.
I pluck weeds to free the growing beets

and as my fingers touch the dew-soaked soil,
I envision roots growing out of my fingers.

Summer when my heart breaks

a birch leaf face down on the road
a belief in the strength of blood
a blue patch, swirls of clouds
accumulation of raindrops
a grief unidentified
a longing for space and silence

a rosebud before it's a rosebud
a meeting of deer in the garden at three in the morning

a taste of the fiery radish root
avenging the deer with rotten scent
a wind carrying smoke

bird joy in early light
boisterous tulips that will wilt by morning
burning back in noonday sun

Canada geese uninterpreted,
        carved into steel sky, chain of checkmarks
        combing for signs, landmarks
craving what cannot be had

dancing with the fireflies
drinking rhubarb wine with new salad greens

each day cracking open a different way
empty space where the gladiolus bulb never grew
every grass blade translucent with green

filled with ecstatic laughter
flat land only in places, naming the mountains
forever the fragrance of deep woods
fragments of memory like lightning

geraniums rimming the flowerbeds
grackles gorged on berries
grief of the days shortening

heart unraveling with heat
heartrending azure sky, fierce and bold

in the calm winds, clear reds, greens, blues
        is there a question that cannot be answered?

laughing alone from sheer wonder
lupines finally allowed to breathe their blue breath

milk seeping from leaves when you snap them
mountains lacking snow, covered in sky
my heart slippery with dew

naming tender flora in the woods
        never lost among the ferns
        none of the flowers knowing my name

oblong shadows at end of day
occasional hummingbirds perching to feed
odd striped insects overtaking the squash leaves
over and over, the flight of the goldfinch

part of nature's medley
pelted with hail, alive
pink going brown around the edges
prayer of wind heard in single syllables

quantities of prickly weeds turning flowery purple
quiet between chirps and breaths

red-winged blackbird screeching in the grass
roads covered in heart-shaped leaves

saplings gaining strength quietly
slim reeds protecting cattails in the swamp
sparrow leaning into storm winds
swinging willow

tenting caterpillars doing the hunger work
twitching cat tail
two praying mantises, their triangular heads
the 5 a.m. sky streaked with roses
trust is a rope, a drum, a cow, a tall pine

under clouds, the happiness of parched grass
until evening the strength of day

visiting the garden with the rabbits
visible vibrations of vegetable life

was that the monarch butterfly signaling the end?
with ignorance we shall live on
      were it not for the true moment singing
      were it not for the stopping of time inside
      were it not for the purple blue curtain of transcendence

      x-ing out the world as we see it hear it smell it

yearning for rapture
years spent seeking
you walked a long way for this

zen

About the Author

Michelle Demers holds an MFA in writing from the Vermont College of Fine Arts and teaches poetry and writing at the Community College of Vermont. She also leads her own workshops, First Thoughts Writing Workshops, regionally. Her chapbook *Epicenter* won the 2006 Blue Light Poetry Prize. Michelle lives and writes in Williston, Vermont, with her brilliant husband and exceptional cat. She is inspired by Vermont's spectacular countryside as well as the deep spiritual questions of life.

www.ingramcontent.com/pod-product-compliance
Lightning Source LLC
Chambersburg PA
CBHW032034090426
42741CB00006B/805